Selling Insurance
with NLP

Selling Insurance with NLP

Advance Psychological
Techniques for Creating
Sales Breakthroughs

Jayden Chen

PARTRIDGE
A Penguin Random House Company

To all insurance sales professionals who worked tirelessly to bring peace of mind, financial security, and happiness to the lives of families they have touched.

To order additional copies of this book, contact
Toll Free 800 101 2657 (Singapore)
Toll Free 1 800 81 7340 (Malaysia)
orders.singapore@partridgepublishing.com

www.partridgepublishing.com/singapore

Contents

Chapter Nine
Handling Objections by Pacing and Reframing

Chapter Ten
The Three-Step BAA Closing Process

Acknowledgements

I wish to thank my NLP trainers for helping me develop the knowledge and skills that made me the adept practitioner I am today. My gratitude also goes to all the insurance salespersons with whom I have come to work; your feedback and contributions have allowed me to gain invaluable insight into both the selling aspect and the application of NLP in insurance products.

Finally, and most important, I would like offer my deepest appreciation to my family for their constant support and unwavering belief in me.

Introduction

NLP and Insurance Selling

In any type of profession, there are two sets of skills which determine how well a person performs: hard skills and soft skills. Hard skills refer to a person's knowledge of the job and occupational skills. On the other hand, soft skills refer to a person's character traits and the interpersonal skills that characterize the person's relationships with other people.

Take a doctor, for instance:, the hard skills required of doctors would be medical knowledge, including a comprehensive understanding of anatomy and physiology, a wide comprehension of illnesses, and the ability to interpret results to give their patients a diagnosis. The soft skills that a doctor is expected to have may include patience, empathy, good listening skills, and politeness.

Similarly, professional salespeople should have hard skills that include a comprehensive knowledge of their own and their competitors' products, operation processes, and claim procedures; they should possess soft skills such as the ability to build rapport, gain trust, detect and respond according to changes in moods and emotions, understand needs and wants, and ensure that their prospects feel at ease and comfortable with them. While hard skills can be acquired and perfected over time, soft skills are more challenging to learn and change. Neuro-linguistic programming, or NLP, has been proven to be the ultimate tool in improving both hard and soft skills, especially soft skills. This is because our soft skills are to a large extent made up of our character traits and the attributes that influence how we interact and deal with other people. NLP, being a study of how our minds work, will be immensely effective in this regard.

You will find NLP skills particularly useful in the sale of insurance products due to most products' inherent complexity. Many insurance products contain long lists of complicated features, terms, and conditions, and they can be extremely intimidating – even for us as sellers, let alone our prospects. Hence, top insurance sellers must not only have a clear understanding of their products but also excellent communication skills to explain their products in a way that their prospects can easily comprehend.

The key to successful insurance selling also hinges upon our ability to build trust with our prospects and to match our product benefits to their needs. In order to do so, we must have the ability to see the world through our prospects' eyes – to see what they see, hear what they hear, and feel what they feel. In other words, we must be able to put ourselves in their shoes. This ability necessitates a high degree of empathy and a profound understanding of people's buying psychology. This is where NLP truly shines.

What is NLP?

NLP stands for Neuro-linguistic programming. It is the study of how we think, feel, and act. NLP practitioners have developed a set of tools and powerful methodologies designed to help us help ourselves and others to achieve personal breakthroughs, understand and influence a change in behaviours and mind-sets, and solicit desired outcomes through subconscious verbal and non-verbal techniques. In the context of insurance selling, NLP arms us with highly effective communication skills to build rapport with our prospects, effect a change in their perception, arouse the desired emotions, and motivate them into taking action.

To appreciate why NLP is such a powerful tool, let us first understand what the terms *neuro*, *linguistic*, and *programming* mean.

Neuro refers to our neurology (the brain or mind), through which our experiences are processed via our five senses:

- visual (see)
- auditory (hear)
- kinaesthetic (feel)
- olfactory (smell)
- gustatory (taste)

Linguistic refers to how language and non-verbal communication (such as body language) are coded, ordered, and given meaning through neural representations. This includes:

- pictures
- sounds
- feelings
- tastes
- smells
- words (self-talk)

Programming refers to the belief that our brains metaphorically operate like computers in the way they process and store information. This explains why different people perceive the same things differently. Besides their physical composition, our brains are made up of a set of programs that help us interpret events and what they mean to us (e.g., does this insurance plan benefit me?) and in turn help us decide how we ought to feel (e.g., should I trust you?) and what action we should take (e.g., should I buy?)

By harnessing the power of NLP and applying them in your insurance sales process you will be able to accomplish the following.

- Quickly establish close rapport with your prospects.
- Use effective listening skills, words, and non-verbal communication to build unwavering trust.
- Employ techniques to elicit the desired outcomes from your prospect.
- Pace and lead your prospects to the point of buying.
- Turn a *no* into a sales opportunity.
- Close the deal quickly and successfully.

History of NLP

Dr Richard Bandler, a mathematician with a strong background in gestalt therapy, and Dr John Grinder, an accomplished professor of linguistics, developed NLP in the mid-1970s. Since then, NLP has been used as an approach to <u>communication</u>, <u>personal development</u>, and <u>psychotherapy</u>. Its creators claim a connection between the neurological processes ("neuro"), language ("linguistic"), and behavioural patterns learned through experience ("programming"), and they claim that these patterns can be changed to achieve specific goals in life. They collaborated in a study with three world-class therapists who were at that time among the most innovative and successful practitioners: Dr Fritz Perls, a psychotherapist and developer of gestalt therapy; Dr Virginia Satir, founder of conjoint family therapy and an expert at resolving the most difficult of family situations; and Dr Milton Erickson, a medical doctor, psychiatrist, and world-renowned clinical hypnotherapist.

Before joining the University of California, Santa Cruz, as a professor of linguistics, Dr Grinder worked as a specialist in the Central Intelligence Agency (CIA) in the Middle East, where he used his expertise in linguistics to gather often sensitive intelligence from the Arabic-speaking communities. Dr Grinder's work is documented in well over 1,000 other educational books on subject matter ranging from specialist NLP topics to psychology, sales, negotiation, management, parenting, and accelerated learning.

Dr Bandler obtained a <u>BA</u> degree in <u>philosophy</u> and <u>psychology</u> from the <u>University of California, Santa Cruz,</u> in 1973, and an <u>MA</u> degree in psychology from <u>Lone Mountain College</u> in <u>San Francisco</u> in 1975. Dr Grinder is a consultant to many Fortune 500 companies, the US Military, US Intelligence Agencies, Major League baseball teams, NFL players, and Olympic athletes.

Chapter One

Understanding Your Prospect

What you see and what you hear depends a great deal on where you are standing. It also depends on what sort of person you are.
—C. S. Lewis

Have you ever wondered why some people simply could not see your point of view, regardless of how rational, logical, and persuasive you thought your point was? The answer is simple: *they don't see your point the way you see it.* People have different ways of seeing things. The way we perceive events, interpret information, and make decisions varies in a way that is predetermined and entrenched by the environment we grew up in, the information we were exposed to, the culture we live in, the teachings we received, and the personal experiences we went through. As the saying goes, "We all live in our own world".

Your Prospect's Representation System

NLP dictates that, fundamentally, a person perceives and experiences the world through five senses: visual (what we see), auditory (what we hear), kinaesthetic (what we feel), olfactory (what we smell), and gustatory (what we taste). In NLP, this is known as our *representational system*. However, in the real world only three of these five representation system are dominant in our day-to-day lives: visual, auditory, and kinaesthetic. In other words, these are the most commonly used senses through which we experience and interpret events.

These representation systems further communicate information to us via two sources: external (things we see, hear, touch, or feel) and internal (things we imagine, think, or feel). For example, in your visual mode, you could actually see beautiful flowers with your eyes, but you could also visualize these images in your mind. In auditory mode, you could listen to a conversation taking place or you could listen to your own self-talk. You could engage your kinaesthetic sense to touch and feel a warm cup of tea, or you could feel the sensation of hunger or fullness in you.

Most people have a preference or tendency to rely on one method more than others; this is called their *primary representational system.* NLP practitioners categorize people as visual-oriented, auditory-oriented, or kinaesthetic-oriented individuals. Once we have so classified our audience, we can then communicate more effectively with them through their primary representation system.

Most of us would agree that people *like* us when they *are like* us. One effective way to build rapport with your prospects is to identify their primary representational system and then quite literally speak their language with them.

Complicated as it may seem, identifying a prospect's primary representation system is actually quite straightforward. Most people will signal their preferred way of experiencing the world through the words they choose, their eye movements, and certain subtle non-verbal signs in their body language.

However, please resist the temptation to put people into "boxes". When we say, "This person is totally kinaesthetic" or "I'm a one-hundred-per-cent visual", we are more apt to make mistakes. More often than not, we use more than one representation system simultaneously. Sometimes we use one more than the others, and sometimes we engage only one completely. It depends on what situation we are in or what information we need to interpret. Having said that, we still can rely on the fact that more often than not most people stick to their preferred mode of thinking. Switching from one system to the other is exhausting; this is not how we are wired to function.

Visual (V)

Visual people look at the world through visual images. They interpret and derive meaning from information by forming images in their minds. They literally *see* everything you are saying in their minds. They are often gazing over your head or off to one side while in a conversation with you; they are not trying to be rude, and this is not a sign of disinterest. Rather, they are processing what you are saying in visual form, looking at the pictures or movies they are creating while you are speaking. They've probably also cast you as the lead in that movie.

When dealing with visual people, remember that "a picture is worth a thousand words". Generously use illustrations to drive home points in your presentations. Show your prospects colourful brochures and sales kits. Visually describe your product's benefits to them to arouse their interest and keep their attention. Visual people are also inclined to "judge a book by its cover" and form a lasting impression at first sight. When dealing with a visual person, remember that appearances matter. Suit up or dress professionally for an appointment with them. Studies have shown that most people form an impression of the person they meet for the first time in the first ten seconds. We all know how tenacious first impressions can be. They are hard to change.

In order for visual people to buy your product, they must be able to visualize themselves enjoying the benefits of owning the product or experience. You should also help them envision the consequences they will face if they choose not to buy. In our context where the product is an insurance plan, you must help them see as vividly as possible the smiles on their families' faces due to the sense of security and peace of mind provided by the insurance product they bought, as well as their grieving faces as a result of having no financial protection upon the prospect's untimely death. These mental pictures will evoke a strong emotional response in your prospects, which will, in turn, prod them into making a decision to buy without any delay.

People who are visual often have an erect posture. They tend to stand or sit with their heads and bodies erect and their eyes straight ahead. They also usually lack patience. Look closely, and you will notice they are often breathing from the tops of their chests. They tend to be organized, neat, and well-groomed. They remember by seeing images and are less distracted by noise. They often have trouble remembering verbal instructions or learning from solely auditory sources such as audiobooks. Instead they prefer to read and see things for themselves.

Auditory (A)

Auditory people are deliberate and exacting in their spoken word, often with pronounced movement of their lips. They are more dynamic in their usage of the tone and pitch of their voices. They are especially attentive to speeches. They remember verbal sequences easily and excel in learning through auditory methods of teaching. They love music and sound. They are able to hear different tones, timbre, cadence, sounds, and words. They can be easily distracted by noise.

They tend to move their eyes sideways while listening to you, as if they are absorbing every word you say. They often turn their heads and point their ears at you to receive your words as clearly as they can. You may notice them breathing from the centres of their chests. Self-talk is common for them, as they make sense of their thoughts by listening to themselves. As opposed to visual people who memorize something in the form of images, auditory people prefer to do it through procedures, steps, and sequences. They like following the rules.

They are good listeners, and they pay attention when you speak. They will accept your ideas or suggestions if they "sound right". Memories are triggered by songs they heard or conversations they held. They spend hours on the phone and like to ask for feedback. Rather than seeing for themselves, they prefer to hear what you think.

Selling to auditory people entails the use of the right tone of voice, a good pace, and apt words. Once they feel that something doesn't sound right, you are out of the door. Illustrations will be helpful, but nothing is as persuasive as a good set of emotion-triggering words. Tell them that if they buy this insurance, they will hear the joy and appreciative words of their loved ones. The reward of hearing "Thank you for planning for our future" is much more appealing to them than the condemnation and disappointment of "Why didn't you plan for our future?"

Kinaesthetic (K)

Kinaesthetic people are those who process information by getting a feel for things and people. These people get information primarily from touch, emotions, gut feelings, and hunches. They need to squeeze a fruit, poke a fish, and feel a garment. They like to pick things up and play with them before they decide to buy (or not). While making a point, they love to touch people to feel a sense of connectedness. They often take their time to process thoughts. They may appear to think more slowly than the other two groups, but they are far from being intellectually inferior. They just need more time for their intuition to arrive. Prospects who often look down during your presentation are just getting a feel of what you are presenting. They are trying to assess their feelings.

The posture of a kinaesthetic can seem sluggish. It may appear that they are never in a hurry, to the extent that they appear to be always dragging their feet about things. They tend to breathe from the bottoms of their lungs, also known as belly breathing.

Selling to kinaesthetic people requires the personal touch. You can't work with these people over the phone, e-mails, or texts. They need to meet you in person, shake your hand, and get a feel for who you are – and whether you can be trusted. Give them something they can hold in their hands, such as a brochure or flyer. Be patient with them; they tend to make short pauses while speaking. For example:

Seller: "What do you think about this product?"

Prospect: "Well, I feel … hmm … it's a rather good … and interesting product."

Never try to rush them; they will see you as pushy and impolite. It is important that you realize they need more time to process information and feel what they think.

Determining Your Prospects' Preferred Representation System

NLP practitioners basically employ three methods to gauge whether a person is visual, auditory, or kinaesthetic in their orientation. First, we notice their preferred predicates in conversations. Second, we pay close attention to their eye movements, which is called eye-accessing cues. And third, we observe their external characteristics, such as how much they talk, their posture, how fast they speak, and the pitch of their voice.

Predicates

Predicates are sensory-based words and phrases that indicate a person's preferred representation. They suggest the activity of seeing, hearing, or feeling, such as "I see what you mean" (visual), "This is unheard of" (auditory), or "I couldn't grasp what you just said" (kinaesthetic). By being a "predicate detective", you will be able to determine which is your prospects' preferred representation systems, and by using their preferred predicates in your conversation with them, you will help them better understand what you are trying to say and enhance your rapport with them. Below are some examples of sensory-based words and phrases for your reference.

List of Predicate Words and Phrases		
Visual	**Auditory**	**Kinaesthetic**
picture	hear	know
show	ask	tackle
see	resonate	hit
clear	mention	affect
look	speak	rub
envision	ring	touch
perceive	tone	feel
view	say	grab
survey	tell	handle
watch	static	grasp
preview	sound	impress
perspective	express	suffer
illustrate	accent	pressure
focus	remark	intuit
reflect	inquire	smooth operator
bright	talk	so-so
sight for sore eyes	unheard of	start from scratch
take a peek	utterly	stiff upper lip
illuminate	voiced out	get a handle on
tunnel vision	well-informed	get a load of
under your nose	within hearing	get in touch with
shed light on	give an account of	get the drift of
get a perspective on	lend me your ears	hand in hand
hazy idea	I am all ears	hang in there
in light of	grant an audience	heated argument
in person	heard voices	hold it
in view of	hidden message	hold on
looks like	hold your tongue	hot-headed
make a scene of	inquire into	know-how

mental picture	loud and clear	lay all cards on the table
mind's eye	manner of speaking	pull some strings
naked eye	power of speech	slipped my mind
paint a picture	purrs like a kitten	too much of a hassle
see to it	state your purpose	can't get a grasp of
short-sighted	to tell the truth	impressed upon
far-sighted	tongue-tied	feels wrong
foresight	clear as a bell	it hit me
foresee	word for word	it dawned on me
upfront	doesn't sound right	deep down
beyond a shadow of a doubt	ring a bell	feels empty

Eye-Accessing Cues

The second key method of determining a person's preferred representation system is to pay attention to his or her eye movements during a conversation. Bandler and Grinder did a videotape study and found a connection between how people think and how their eyes move. This observation is further reinforced by neurological research showing that eye movements both laterally and vertically seem to activate different parts of the brain. In NLP, these eyes movements give us insights as to how people are accessing information.

However, one person differs from another, and our reactions, although generally predictable, could be unique to us. One must not allow eye-accessing cues to be the sole determining factor in assessing a person's representation system. It should only be used as a starting point and one of the cues which must be read together with other cues. Although it may not tell us the entire story, it will give us an educated guess or a hunch about what is going on. Utilizing the eye-accessing cues, nonetheless, has its benefit: it forces us to stay alert and pay close attention to our prospects, which in turn helps us pick up on other cues.

Eye-Accessing Cues and Rapport

Rapport is most important, and it is the very first thing we need to establish with our prospects in order to build trust. Only a trusting relationship between prospect and seller will lead to a successful sales process. One of the best ways to build trust with your prospects is to "speak their language", and eye-accessing cues will give you a good start in ascertaining which representation system you prospect is inclined toward.

For instance, if you have a prospect who frequently moves his or her eyes to the "up left" or "up right", he is most likely processing the information by creating mental pictures in his or her mind or recalling images he or she has seen before. Knowing he or she is probably a visual person, you could now use illustrations and sprinkle visual predicates throughout your presentation. By doing this, you will be able to build close rapport with your prospect faster than ever before.

> *When the eyes say one thing, and the tongue another, a practiced man relies on the language of the first.*
> —Ralph Waldo Emerson

Eye-Accessing Cues	
Visual: Eyes centre (defocused)/up left/up right This is where we usually look when we are recalling images we have seen before. For example, the face of our spouse, the last restaurant we dined at, or the colour of the shirt we wore last Friday.	
Auditory: Eyes to the left side or right side (horizontal) This is where we usually look when we are recalling sounds that we heard before. For example, our mother's voice or a favourite song.	

Kinaesthetic: Eyes down and to right This is where we will usually look when we are experiencing feelings. For example, how we felt when we got that first car, or how we felt when we won a lucky draw.	
Auditory-Digital (or Self-Talk): Eyes down and to left This is where we usually look when talking to ourselves or asking questions in our heads.	

Note: Left-handed people may have a reversed pattern from left to right. This means that their eyes accessing cues are the mirror image of those of the right hander. When accessing a feeling, they will look down and left, instead of down and right.

Visual Characteristics

People with a strong preference for one type of representation system may display certain visual characteristics peculiar to that group. Following are some good signs to look out for.

Visual Characteristics	Auditory Characteristics	Kinaesthetic Characteristics
• maintains good eye contact • high-pitched voice • moves, thinks, and talks fast • good with directions • good visual memory • trouble recalling verbal instructions • stands upright • breathes from the top of the chest	• low-pitched voice • rhythmic and smooth • sounds good • loves concerts and music • self-talk • learns by listening • can repeat things accurately back to you • breathes from centre of the chest • frequent internal dialogue	• frequent pauses in conversation • likes to touch people • talks and breathes slowly • responds to touch • memorizes by doing • breathes from lower abdomen

• nicely dressed and well-groomed • tidy and dislikes clutter	• memorizes by steps, procedures, sequences • tends to lean back • slow to respond	

Your Own Representational System

Knowing your own preferred representational system helps you better understand the way you communicate with your prospects and allows you to tailor your system to match your prospect's system. This avoids what we call a "clash of representational systems" that could stop you from getting your point across.

Take the *Representational System Preference Test* below to learn what your preferred mode of thinking is. This test is by no means conclusive, as each person's preferred representational system changes over time and in different contexts. You should go through the test every few months. There is no right or wrong answer, and one representational system is not superior to another. It merely provides you an added insight on how you prefer to communicate with others (and yourself). The mode you score the highest in is your favourite. The mode you score the lowest in is your least favourite, although you can communicate in all three modes.

Visual/Auditory/Kinaesthetic Representational System Preference Test		
In the list below, check A, B, or C, depending on which response appeals to you the most. The mode you score highest in indicates your preference.		
1.	A		I like listening to music or playing musical instruments.
	B		I like to draw.
	C		I like to touch or poke something before I buy it.

2.	A		I think I express myself better verbally.
	B		I remember words easily and could spell them out accurately most of the time.
	C		I tend to deal with issues using my intuition.
3.	A		I like listening to my voice and always try to make it sound good.
	B		I try to look my best because it gives me confidence.
	C		I like to touch others while talking to them.
4.	A		I find talking about issues helps me resolve them.
	B		I like concepts to be explained with illustrations.
	C		I want to be able to touch and hold the product being sold to me.
5.	A		I am able to detect insincerity or dishonesty through a person's voice.
	B		I judge people by their appearance.
	C		A good or bad handshake matters to me.
6.	A		I would rather listen to the news on the radio than to read the newspaper.
	B		I love to go to the cinema and watch TV.
	C		I like outdoor physical activities.
7.	A		I am good at controlling the volume and tone of my voice when speaking.
	B		My room must be kept tidy and clean.
	C		Comfort is the most important thing for my room.
8.	A		I get compliments for being a good communicator.
	B		I like to observe my surroundings.
	C		I am very comfortable with people's touch.

9.	A		I can recognize voices easily after hearing only once.
	B		I am bad with names but good with recalling people's looks.
	C		I can't remember peoples' faces.
10.	A		I like singing or humming along with the radio.
	B		I like taking photos.
	C		I like to be hands-on when learning something.
11.	A		I prefer people explaining things to me rather than showing me images.
	B		I understand and remember better when shown illustrations.
	C		I like to be involved in something rather than just watching.
12.	A		I listen patiently.
	B		An appearance leaves a lasting impression with me.
	C		I can have sensitive feelings towards others without knowing why.
13.	A		I like to think out loud.
	B		I am good with using maps.
	C		I like to pamper myself after a long day's work.
14.	A		I like a quiet room or area in my house designated for listening to music.
	B		I like see my work desk uncluttered and organized.
	C		Comfort is my priority when buying a car.
15.	A		I am good at imitating people's voices.
	B		I motivate myself by keeping inspiring pictures in my surroundings.
	C		I like to learn things through a detailed, step-by-step process.

Count and write down the number of A, B, and C responses below. The response with the highest score indicates your preferred representational system.

Responses	Number	Preference
A		Auditory
B		Visual
C		Kinaesthetic

My preferred representational
system is _____.

Chapter Two

Building Trust through Verbal Communication

The toughest thing about the power of trust is that it's very difficult to build and very easy to destroy. The essence of trust building is to emphasize the similarities between you and the customer.

—Thomas J. Watson

In the first chapter, I have expounded the three primary representational systems and how these groups may perceive and experience the world differently from us. We have also learned how to recognize these individuals through three methods: eye-accessing cues, the predicates they use, and their visual characteristics. Once you are able to tell which group your prospect belongs to, you should never see it as an impediment but rather an advantage. This is because you can now tailor your communication style to match the prospect's, and this will not only give you better rapport and trust with your prospect but also make you better able to enthuse him or her about your products.

Visual Prospects

Visual people are usually well groomed. They move, think, and speak fast with a high-pitched voice. They tend to sprinkle visual words or predicates all over their conversation. When we use similar predicates while talking to them – words like *picture, see, show, envision, reflect*, and *in light of* – they take an instant liking to us and will start to trust us because they feel we understand them.

Using predicates is not difficult; in fact, it can become second nature with some practice in your daily presentations to your prospects. Below are some examples of how you could use visual predicates or words. I have given examples for different types of insurance products to help you better understand and learn how to use them.

- "Mr. Wane, just *picture* how difficult life would be for your family if you were to die without enough protection for them."
- "I bet you can *see* the benefits our plan offers."
- "Try to *envision* how satisfied you will feel knowing you have made a right decision for your family today."
- "I hope I have *shed a light* on the importance of this plan for your family and yourself."
- "Can you *imagine* the hefty bills, not to mention the pain you would have to endure, if you were hospitalized for critical illnesses.
- "Facts clearly *show* the importance of saving now for our futures."
- "Mr. Wane, allow me to *give you a preview* of the benefits our plan offers."
- "I hope you can *reflect* on the possibility of having insufficient funds for the future and thus being a burden to your children."
- "We *foresee* an inflation hike in the coming years. Therefore, we must start saving now."
- "Disciplined savings from now will secure your children's *bright* future."
- "*Seeing* consistent income coming from our annuity plan later will be the best thing you will experience in retirement."

Besides using visual words or predicates, you can enhance your presentations to visually-based prospects with brochures, tables, images, and interesting sales materials. Using visual aids is very effective in a presentation, and especially so when dealing with people in this mode. You save them the extra step of "translating" your information into their familiar mode of representation, and thus you allow them concentrate on the message you are trying to convey. For example, if you based your presentation on an auditory-oriented style while speaking to visual prospects, words you use might sound strange to them. As a result, they can't help but translate everything you say to their preferred mode, and this unavoidably disrupts their understanding of your presentation.

Due to the complicated nature of most insurance plans – at least for a layperson – most top insurance sellers illustrate their plans by drawing and writing on a blank sheet of paper. This is very helpful for most customers, more so for the visuals. You don't have to be an artist to do this. Simply repeat some illustrations you have learned earlier in your training. This is a good place to start to learn. However, it is crucial that you make it clear to your prospect that the drawings done by you are not meant to be official materials but merely an informal representation of the information. Prospects should always be told to rely on the official and approved materials from your company, such as brochures, sales materials, approved quotations, or sales illustrations.

> *A smart salesperson listens to emotions, not facts.*
> — Unknown

Auditory Prospects

Auditory people learn more through listening than through other methods of perception. They like listening to radios rather than TVs, and audiobooks rather than conventional books. When speaking to auditory-oriented prospects, include auditory predicates or words, as well as words that evoke an emotional response. You need a good set of vocabulary to arouse their interest and get them to take action. Here are some examples.

- "Wouldn't it *sound* great if you could *tell* your family that they are financially well-protected if something untoward were to happen to you?"
- "Ever *heard* of people complaining how costly retirement life can be? Does it *ring a bell*?"
- "If you would *lend me your ears*, this plan will certainly *sound* beneficial to you and your family."
- "The type of benefits offered by my plan is certainly *unheard* of in the industry."
- "*Speaking* from a professional insurance seller's point of view, I think the assured sum you need is a lot higher."
- "Imagine the gratitude you will *hear* from your loved ones after you have bought this plan for them."
- "Doesn't *hearing* about other people's remorse for not saving for retirement earlier in their life worry you?"
- "Mr. Wane, feel free to tell me your concerns. *I am all ears.*"

Try using powerful vocabulary and emotional words to galvanize your prospects into taking action. Here are some examples.

- "Imagine the *agony and anguish* your family would have to go through without enough protection."
- "Their lives would be filled with *sorrow* and *misery* if something unfortunate were to happen to you."
- "If you passed away without enough insurance, you would leave your loved ones feeling *disappointed*, *dismal,* and *dejected*."
- "By making a decision today, you will make your family *feel safe and secure*."

You can still use illustrative materials effectively with auditory prospects if you combine them with a clearer and detailed explanation. The difference between auditory and visual prospects is that the former may take a slightly longer time to absorb the visual information, as they need to "translate" it to their preferred auditory form for better understanding. They may need to read it to themselves in the form of self-talk, so you should pass them the materials and leave it with them for a while before proceeding to give a verbal explanation.

To sell to auditory prospects, you also need to pay extra attention to where you meet them. Try to meet these sound-sensitive prospects at a quiet location, as noise can be a serious distraction for them. They will get agitated by loud music or road noise, and as a result they will find themselves hardly able to concentrate on your presentation. If music is unavoidable, choose a venue with slow music. Slow music helps your customer relax, so they will be able to listen patiently to what you have to say. In fact, you may actually benefit from soothing music playing at the background, because it helps calm your anxiety and prevents you from rushing through your presentation.

Kinaesthetic Prospects

Selling to a kinaesthetic takes a lot of personal touch, and they welcome this and often find it comforting provided you have already established a basic level of rapport with them. A light touch with your hands on their arm when you emphasize a point, or a light pat on their back to prod them into making a decision will go a long way in helping you secure a deal.

Bringing along sales materials such as brochures is of paramount importance when meeting kinaesthetic prospects. However, merely looking at documents will not do it for them; they need to grab and flip through the material to get a feel of what they are looking at – something you should encourage. Give them a calculator to do the calculations themselves, pass them the drawings you have done, and let them hold them while you explain what it's about. This helps them get a good grasp of the points you are trying to make.

As with the other two representation systems, the use of predicates will go a long way to help you seal the deal. Here are some examples.

- "Mr. Wane, let me help you *make sense* of what I am trying to say."
- "This illustration will help you get a *good grasp* of the benefits offered in my plan."
- "Imagine how *delighted* you will *feel* when you know your family will be well taken care of in the event of any mishap."

- "After you have put your signature here on the dotted line, you are guaranteed *peace of mind*."
- "We all *know deep down* that we need to force ourselves to save early in life."
- "After seeing the facts I present, doesn't it *dawn on you* that you may not be financially prepared for retirement?"
- "If you decide today, your family will be *comforted* to know that you have planned for them."
- "My presentation today will give you a *concrete idea* of what you need."

Kinaesthetic types are by far the easiest to convince of their need for insurance plans; this is simply because insurance selling depends predominantly on our ability to elicit the necessary buying emotions from our prospects. Buying insurance can be both a pleasant and a sad experience; it provides peace of mind, but it reminds us of the fact that we are all mortal.

Group Selling

If you have more than one person in your meeting, the chances are that you will have to use more than one type of representation system in your sales pitch. This is not as difficult as it may seem. All you need to do is use all three modes of representation throughout your presentation. If you fail to do so, you will be neglecting some people in your audience and you will fail to create the desired impact.

When speaking to your audience, you could use one predicate after another in subsequent sentences, such as this:

"By *looking* at the slides in front of you, you will *see* the enormous benefits offered by our plan. And if you could *lend me an ear*, you will agree with me that it's the best plan you can ever have. Now, just *imagine* your wife and children thanking you for planning for their future and being such a *thoughtful* and *caring* father. *Ask* yourself an honest question: does my family need this plan? Your *conscience* will tell you yes! You should *listen* to your *gut feeling* and make a decision today. After the decision, you will have *a sense of relief* knowing that your loved ones will *feel safe* and *secure* in the event that you suffer any mishap."

What I have done here is include predicates or words for all three modes – visual, auditory, and kinaesthetic – into one short presentation.

It is also paramount to utilize presentation aides targeted at all three representation systems, or you risk losing them along the way. Slide presentations, background music, and activities such as raising hands to answer questions and allowing them time to jot down what they heard are all good ways to stimulate their interest and retain it. Let me share with you how I use slide presentations effectively in sales presentations with a group. To target visual audiences, I insert colours, images, shapes, and graphs in my slides. To target auditory audiences, I play background music before I start and during breaks; you could also add sound effects for between the slide transitions and when you click on your mouse. With kinaesthetic audiences, I ask and encourage them to raise their hands to answer questions, I distribute printed copies of relevant sales materials and let them hold them and write on them, and I bring along brochures or sales materials and pass everybody a copy. To ensure a kinaesthetic audience stays attentive, you may also walk up to them and pat some of them on the shoulder or shake their hands. This creates good rapport between the audience and the speaker. However, it's best to do this before the talk starts and while they are entering the room. This way you will shake everyone's hand and won't miss out on any touch-sensitive people.

Selling to Pairs

A slightly different approach is used when presenting only to two people. You start by studying which representational system each prefers. For example, the husband may prefer visual and the wife kinaesthetic. In this case, you will need to keep going back and forth, speaking to each person in turn and using the appropriate mode. It is very much like presenting to a large group or audience, save that you probably only need to stick to two modes here. Needless to say, if you were oblivious and ended up presenting your product in one mode – visual, for example, in this case – the wife would feel left out and more likely than not would dissuade her husband from buying because she *felt something was not right*.

Just remember to remain alert and flexible. Constantly read your prospects' cues and switch your modes as you see shifts in your prospects. Although they may prefer to use a particular mode most of the time, they do move from one mode to the other depending on the environment and the situation they are in. Therefore, be careful not to assume a person is entirely in one mode or unable to change mode. There is no such thing as a completely visual, completely auditory, or completely kinaesthetic person. People are just more inclined to use one mode than the other, or they may be stronger in one than in the other.

Chapter Three

Rapport and Trust Building

The most important thing in communication
is hearing what isn't said.
—Peter F. Drucker

Rapport and trust go hand in hand. One won't exist without the other. Hence, good rapport skills are vital to the success of a sales process. In NLP, practitioners employ a set of non-verbal communication techniques to make the other person feel comfortable, understood, and relaxed – all the ingredients necessary for fostering a trusting relationship. We call this technique "matching and mirroring". It is basically a conscious effort by us to match and mirror our prospect's non-verbal behaviour, such as their gesture, body language, posture, facial expression, and even their breathing.

As we discussed in Chapter One, "people like those who are like themselves". People are naturally more gravitated towards those who display similar physical or non-physical attributes. This is because they feel they know them, which in turn gives them a sense of security. All this happens, though, at an unconscious or a subconscious level, which means we are unaware of it most of the time. The subconscious decisions or judgements that we make manifest themselves through our responses to the other person, and you may hear yourself saying things like:

- "I really don't trust this person very much."
- "I am not going to buy this because I feel he doesn't know what I really need."
- "I really like him; he seem trustworthy."
- "I feel that he understood my needs very well."
- "I felt like I have known him for a long time."

Showing your prospects that you truly understand them is thus the key to a fruitful relationship.

Mirroring and Matching

Ever noticed a loving couple or two close friends communicating with each other, having a meal together, or just sitting idly next to each? More often than not you will see similar or matching body language or posture between them. Conversely, what if they had an argument and fell out? Will you still see what you just saw? Or will you see a "mismatch"? This is when one deliberately mismatches the other. For instance, one will stand when the other sits or one will lean back as the other leans forwards. These drastic changes are due to the rapport being broken. They are no longer in good terms with each other and therefore don't want to be like each other.

All this happens unconsciously as part of our natural responses to our feelings towards other people. Appreciating how our subconscious minds react to non-verbal behaviours of another person goes a long way towards helping us build trust and good rapport with others – and in our context, with prospects.

Mirroring: You follow your prospect's actions as if you were looking at a mirror. For example, if your prospect crosses the right leg over the left leg, you will mirror him or her by crossing your left leg over your right leg. You are basically doing the same act but using the opposite side of your limbs.

Matching: When your prospect crosses the right leg over the left leg, you match him or her by crossing your right leg over your left leg as well. You are basically, following your prospect's action with exactly the same side of your limbs.

Crossover: This is when you mirror your prospect's gestures with a different part of your body, or do something similar. In other words, if your prospect crosses his or her legs, you cross your arms instead. If your prospect leans back in the seat and clasps hands behind the head, you can lean back and put your hands at your sides. You can tap your pen while your prospect plays with the calculator. This is particularly useful when you find your prospect's gestures difficult to imitate or if you are a female trying to mirror a male's gestures that seem inappropriate. If a male prospect spreads his legs, you can spread your arms instead.

Below is a non-exhaustive list of behaviours and body parts you can mirror and match:

Behaviours You Can Mirror and Match:

- facial expression
- eye contact
- eye squinting
- head tilting
- rate of blinking
- posture
- body gestures (arms, legs, hands, and feet)
- weight distribution (while seated or standing)
- breathing patterns (shallow or deep)
- tone and volume of voice
- speed of speech

Body Parts You Can Match

Whole body: Match or mirror your prospect's posture.

Partial body: Match or mirror habitual gestures such as head nods, shrugs, and hand movements.

Half body: Match or mirror the upper or lower part of your prospect's body, such as standing straight or sideways or distributing weight to one side of the body.

Voice: Match tempo, volume, tone, intensity, and intonation patterns. (This is especially useful over the phone.)

Breathing: Match depth and speed (fast/slow/moderate) and breathing position (high/low/middle, shoulder/stomach/chest).

To avoid your prospects discovering that you are trying to mirror or match them, avoid making exaggerated or grand gestures. Be subtle, make similar but less obvious and abrupt changes.

Matching Breathing Patterns

One of the most powerful tools in non-verbal rapport building is matching the other person's breathing patterns. Done successfully, it's like tuning in to their frequency. A great way to identify your prospect's breathing pattern is by imagining that you are looking past his or her chest rather than straight at it. Pay attention to the depth and rate (speed) of his or her breath with your peripheral (side) vision. Once you are able to match it, you will both feel you have known each other for a long time. Try, and you will see it does indeed work!

Be cautious, however. If you are a man, never stare straight at a lady's chest to watch her pattern. You may end up with a slap in the face for inappropriate behaviour. Instead, as I mentioned earlier, use your peripheral vision to do it.

Matching a person's breathing becomes easy with practice. Some breathe so heavily it is easy to see; some do it less obviously; their breathing is light and slow but still discernible if you pay close attention. The trick is to start noticing and practicing often.

Matching Voice

Take the first few minutes of your meeting to learn your prospect's voice patterns. The way a person speaks reflects their mood, feelings, and thoughts at that moment, and by matching it, you create a sense that both of you are on the same wavelength. Below is how you could decipher your prospect's voice or speaking pattern and make it easier for you to follow.

Pace: This is how fast you speak.,. Some speak faster than others, depending on a variety of factors such as which part of the country they are from and their mother tongue. They could also speak more hastily if they are in a hurry, feeling impatient, or simply excited. So don't jump to conclusions.

Pitch: This is the degree of highness or lowness of a tone—such as low, deep, or high-pitched.

Timbre: This is the sound quality that describes those characteristics of sound which allow the ear to distinguish sounds which have the same pitch and loudness. *Timbre* is then a general term for the distinguishable characteristics of a tone, for example, a full and rich voice which projects into every corner of the room.

Inflections: This refers to how words are said differently by different people, how they are shortened, lengthened, or emphasized. This can be particularly obvious in distinctive accents from different parts of a country or in people with different mother tongues.

Having a voice mismatch with your prospect can be a serious hindrance to great rapport-building. It can be very distracting for your prospect if you speak to him or her in opposing voice patterns. For example, your prospect speaks with a fast and high-pitched voice while you speak in a deep, low, and deliberate tone. This distraction stems from the fact that the prospect needs to adjust to your speaking style in order to grasp what you are saying, which can itself be challenging enough.

Voice matching skills are especially valuable for telemarketers. Do it well, and you will see your how remarkable the results can be. The reason is simple. Your voice is the primary method of communicating rapport when you are on the phone. It is the only communication through which the product information is imparted and your sincerity conveyed. Therefore you must be attuned to your prospect's style of speaking. If your prospect is in a hurry and speaks quickly with a high pitch but you insist on taking your time and explaining yourself slowly, you should expect to be hung up on. If you and your prospects have very different accents, you should try your best to speak like them, or at the very least, if you can't match the accent, speak with as much clarity as possible. If your prospect speaks with a slow, deep voice, slow down your voice and speak deliberately.

Calibration

The word *calibrate* means to make precise measurements. In our context, your capability to calibrate well to your prospect's state of mind, behavioural patterns, and representational systems determines to a significant degree how effective your communication will be with them. You do this by mirroring and matching your prospects' verbal and non-verbal communication. Throughout your presentation, you will review their verbal and non-verbal expressions in the context of their response to see if these expressions are still an accurate representation of their mental state, or they could have changed the meaning attached to their responses.

In other words, folding arms could mean a person is defensive or closed-minded to what you are sharing with them, or it could simply mean they are just comfortable in this posture or feeling cold. To calibrate successfully, we must be patient and respect our prospects as individuals and refrain from jumping to conclusions about the meaning of their outward behaviours. As time passes, your careful observations will help you develop the astute intuition you need.

Be wary not to adopt the "interpretive model" of body language – the sweeping generalization that generally says "this posture means this" or "that look means that". If someone slams his fist on the desk, it is probably a fair guess that he is pretty upset. However, subtle gestures or postures should not be interpreted to mean the same things for all people.

Mismatching

Occasionally, you may find prospects who just can't stop talking, but it is rude to stop them abruptly. What do you do then? You can use the mismatching technique to gently break your prospect's conversation flow or mental state. For example, you can break eye contact with them, turn your body at an angle to them, or breathe faster or slower in contrast to their breathing. This sudden change in your body language will jolt them and bring them back from whatever state of mind they are in.

Remember to get in touch with the way the other person feels. Feelings are 55per cent body language, 38 per cent tone and 7 per cent words.

Chapter Four

Effective Listening to Build Trust

"The most basic of all human needs is the need to understand and be understood. The best way to understand people is to listen to them."
—Ralph Nichols

Ever heard of the saying "I don't care how much you know until I know how much you care"? What it basically means is that your prospects will only trust you enough to buy from you if they are convinced that you care more about fulfilling their needs than your own need to close the sale. So how do we make them feel cared for, that we empathize with them and understand what they need? The answer is simple: stop talking so much, ask more questions, and listen carefully.

Levels of Listening

Fortunately, good listening skills, like all other skills, can be learned. Below are three levels of listening rated according how intently we listen to the other person:

Pretentious Listening: We are all familiar with this sort of listening, and occasionally we may be guilty of it too. It occurs when you pretend to listen to someone talking to you by nodding your head while continuing to read the newspaper, meddle with your phone, or watch TV. Another example is when parents pretend to listen to their children but are occupied with household chores.

> *Listening, not imitation, may be the sincerest form of flattery.*
> —Dr Joyce Brothers

Active Listening: This is widely accepted as the key to effective listening, because it involves the listener in actively listening and responding to the other person. The listener takes an active role in the conversation, listening and talking, listening and talking. This is not our preferred style of listening.

> *There are people who, instead of listening to what is being said to them, are already listening to what they are going to say themselves.*
> —Albert Guinon

Deep Listening: This is a rarely heard-of version of listening skills. At this level, the listener pays close attention to not only what is being said but also what is not. When you are listening deeply, basically you listen more than you speak, often asking probing questions in response to what you hear to gather more information that is not necessarily apparent on the surface. You try to read between the lines. You try to discover the reasons, emotions, and intentions underlying the speaker's remarks. The listener tries to discover his or her world. This is the ultimate listening skill that we should all learn.

> *Listening looks easy, but it's not simple. Every head is a world.*
> —Cuban Proverb

Pretentious listening is the worst thing you can do to your prospect, and it is almost certain to cost you your sale. It is unfortunately pervasive among salespeople. They have an irrepressible need to babble on about their products and have no interest in hearing the concerns of their prospect. They pretentiously acknowledge what their prospect says, for example, by nodding or making sounds like "mm, mm, mm" without putting a thought to what it truly means. Once the prospect has stopped talking, they quickly continue with their presentation without first properly addressing the prospect's concern. The result is that prospects feel that their needs are not heard, and they have no trust in the salesperson.

Active listening, on the other hand, occurs when sellers do pay attention to what the prospects are saying, but they only hear the obvious as they are preoccupied with preparing a response. This way, the salesperson will not be able to find the right solution, as he or she only heard part of the concerns but not the underlying reasons.

To illustrate this, let's imagine a prospect saying to you, "I don't have the budget for this". This could mean a few things, among them:

- The prospect likes the plan but *does not have the money* to buy it.
- The prospect likes the plan and can afford the plan but *feels that it's not worth* paying so much.
- The prospect doesn't see how the plan benefits him, *so he doesn't want it*.

If the salesperson in this case hurriedly prepared an answer instead of asking probing questions to find out more, he or she would have missed the point and lost the deal.

> *The best salespeople are great listeners – that's how you find out what the buyer wants.*
> —Larry Wilson and Spencer Johnson

Salespeople who employ "deep listening" with their prospects will have great influence over the conversation. For the sake of sounding polite and amicable, what we hear is usually a deleted or distorted version of what the prospect true wants to say. For example, you may ask your prospect if she likes the product you are proposing to her, to which she answers, "Yes. I *think* I *quite* like it" out of politeness, but all the while she sounds bored and disinterested. If you paid enough attention, your intuition might tell you that your prospect has actually qualified her seemingly positive answer by using the words *think* and *quite* – both connoting doubts. This may then prompt you to probe further instead of jumping straight to closing before the prospect is ready to buy.

It is therefore up to us to decipher the true meaning behind our prospects' words, and our chances of closing the deal will be greatly diminished by our inability to discover their true needs. This type of listening entails cultivation of great patience and humility in ourselves.

Patient listening is simple but not easy. We think a lot faster than we talk, which explains why we are apt to form preconceptions or jump to conclusions before someone has finished their sentences. However, this skill can be mastered by learning what we call "reflective listening", described in the next section – a step-by-step process to effective listening.

> *Effective listeners remember that "words have no meaning – people have meaning." The assignment of meaning to a term is an internal process; meaning comes from inside us. And although our experiences, knowledge and attitudes differ, we often misinterpret each other's messages while under the illusion that a common understanding has been achieved.*
>
> —Larry Barker

Reflective Listening

Reflective listening is a seemingly non-passive exercise where the salesperson takes an active role in the conversation by listening, acknowledging, reflecting, restating, and confirming the prospect's needs. This helps deepen rapport and trust between the two. It addition to improving rapport and trust, reflective listening also lets you understand your prospects' needs and feelings a lot better. It is done by pacing what your prospects say, by giving them constant feedback, such as "What I understand from your statement is …", or by repeating what they have said to them in your own words – we call this "restating" – and finishing by confirming with them what their needs are. Reflective listening can be summed up by the mnemonic **L.E.A.R.N**

Listen: Listen intently to your prospects. Pay attention not only to what is being said verbally but also non-verbally – through their intonation, body language, gestures, facial expression, and other non-spoken expressions.

Empathize: Empathy means the ability to identify with another's feelings. It is not enough to just listen to what your prospects say; you must look at things from their point of view and put yourself in their shoes. By doing so, you will be able to tailor your presentation to meet their needs or desires.

Acknowledge: Acknowledging your prospects when they are talking means showing that you are listening to them. Giving them responses like "uh huh", "I see", or nodding your head will go a long way to encourage your prospects to speak more, which is critical in deepening trust and rapport.

Reflect and restate: Reflecting on what your prospects have said and restating their thoughts and feelings back to them in your own words is another important step. It assures your prospects that you do understand how they feel. For example, your prospect says, "Someone called me about this sort of plan. He was kind of pushy." You respond by saying, "He is kind of pushy, huh." Or if the prospect says, "The economy is incredibly slow now," you say, "Yeah, it's really slow."

Needs confirmation: The final step in this process is to ensure that both of you are on the same page, that you have correctly figured out your prospect's needs and desires. The surest way to find out is to seek a confirmation from your prospect. This can be done by asking questions like "From what you told me, am I right to say that your number one priority now is to start saving for your children?" or "You urgently need a medical card with comprehensive and high coverage. Am I right?"

The key to successfully applying the **L.E.A.R.N**. principle is patience. The salesperson will need to resist the urge to think "the more you talk, the more likely the prospect will buy". Research has shown that people may very well have made up their minds halfway into a presentation once they discover that a few of the product features being offered meet their needs, and they may not be interested in other features that are not relevant to them. Remember that when the prospect is ready to buy, you must sell! Don't babble on and risk confusing the prospect. Briefly mention other features the product comes with and wrap it up. If you do listen intently to your prospect, you will be able to pick up "buying signals" from your prospect; likewise you may pick up "negative signals" that entail further explanation or clarification on your part. Master the art of listening, and you will be a discerning salesperson who is sensitive to your prospects' needs.

Chapter Five

Powerful Verbal Skills for Insurance Selling

Communication – the human connection – is the key to personal and career success.

—Paul J. Meyer

Be a Word Detective

With the highly effective listening skills you have learned in the previous chapter, you will now learn to be a "word detective", identifying words that carry special meaning for your prospects. People have a tendency to repeatedly using certain words to represent what they want to say or how they feel, and these very words could be associated with certain emotions or feelings that are important to them.

As an astute salesperson, you should listen intently to your prospects, catching these words and using them back in your presentations. By doing this, you make your prospect feel listened to and understood; it is a great rapport builder. This technique resembles the "mirroring and matching" technique you have learned earlier, except that it's in verbal form now. You can call it "verbal mirroring" if you like!

This technique is very simple. Once you hear certain words being repeated frequently by your prospect, you simply repeat these words back to them. For instance, you prospect may say, "I would like to have *rock-solid* protection for my family" at some point during the conversation and then later in the same conversation say, "Premium is not my concern, so long as the protection is *rock-solid*". The keyword here is obviously "rock-solid", and you should include it in your response. For example, you could say, "This insurance plan offers a *rock-solid* protection for your family because …"

Besides being able to identify important words in speech, you must also pay attention to the way your prospects describe something. For instance, you may hear your prospects say, "I prefer a plan that gives me not only protection but also good savings". They use the phrase "good savings" rather than technical insurance terms like "high returns" or "high surrender value". Accordingly, you should use these preferred terms and repeat them in your presentation.

Never try to correct your prospects. Forcing them to use other words may confuse how they feel about your plan or even irritate them. On the contrary, by being flexible and adaptable and using words they like, you will make them feel you have been receptive to them, and in return they will keep an open mind to what you are trying to propose.

Powerful Words and Phrases for Insurance Selling

Words have a profound impact on people's thoughts and feelings. Words can motivate and galvanize someone into action, bring back memories, evoke deep feelings, or arouse emotions. Your prospects will only buy if they have the desire to own the plan, and desire itself is an emotion. Similarly, they will not buy because they *felt* that the plan was of no value to them or their families. If enjoying peace of mind is important to your prospect and the words you choose to use evoke this feeling, you have a good chance of closing the sale. Words that may bring up the feelings of peace of mind would include *financial security*, *protected*, and *sufficiently covered*.

The two words "information" and "communication" are often used interchangeably, but they signify quite different things. Information is giving out; communication is getting through.

—Sydney J. Harris

Following is a list of persuasive words and phrases that you can use in your presentations. They are effective both in verbal and written form, as well as marketing and sales materials.

Powerful Words and Phrases for Insurance Selling
guaranteed
promise
short commitment
long-term benefits
peace of mind
safety net
safe
secure
stable
hope
needs
love
care
family
dependents
protected
covered
sheltered
enjoy
provided for
new
save
health
proven
results
good
best
free

future

discover

benefits

simply

easy

money

retirement income

comfortable

relax

assured

gift

life

Metaphors and Similes for Insurance Selling

When you make an analogy between two things and suggest that one resembles the other, you are using a metaphor to describe something. For example, when you say, "She is the apple of my eye", you don't literally mean that she is in fact an apple in your eye. Instead you mean she is someone you hold dear. Similarly, the expression "He is fishing in troubled waters" does not mean the person is fishing literally, but rather, he is searching or trying to gain something in a difficult situation.

As insurance is a non-tangible, highly abstract product. It is unlike selling a car or a microwave where your prospect can actually touch and feel what they will be buying. Buying insurance entails the prospect being able to conceive the idea the seller is trying to promote, which is why insurance is often characterized as "concept-selling".

The benefits of using metaphors are numerous. They can help simplify complex subjects, aid in the listeners' understanding, make something memorable, make the listener more receptive to fresh ideas, and elicit the necessary emotions and feelings. Below are some examples of how you can use metaphors and similes to effectively bring home a point to your prospect.

- "The protection provided is a safety net, catching you and your family if you fall."
- "Having enough insurance is like having enough lifeboats on your ship – enough to rescue you and your loved ones if the boat sinks."
- "The difference between our product and others in the market is like a car with seven air bags and one with only two. We give you enough protection."
- "Imagine that you have an invisible and enormous umbrella above you and your family all the time, sheltering you in your time of need."Many find the burden of paying their monthly mortgage or housing loan quickly disappeared as their income grew. The same is true for paying for your insurance."
- "Having a comprehensive medical insurance plan is similar to having a well-stocked first-aid kit at home – just in case."
- "The importance of insurance can be understood by asking ourselves why we put a spare tire in our car – because we won't know when we need it, but we absolutely must have it!"
- "The restrictive nature of insurance saving plans is in fact an intrinsic benefit. Remember how our parents forced us to save in piggy banks when we were kids? Once in, it's hard to get it out again. It's called disciplined savings."

Metaphor is a tool used not just by top sales professionals but also by eloquent politicians, teachers, coaches, and CEOs. There is no standard formula to create a good metaphor. As long as it's easy to understand (so that even a child could comprehend it), it's probably a good one. Start inventing some metaphors for the insurance plans you are selling, customize them to fit the points you want to make, and most important, start practicing them in your daily presentations. Your prospects will definitely find your presentation much more interesting and exciting.

The ability to simplify means to eliminate the unnecessary so that the necessary may speak.

—Hans Hofmann

Chapter Six

Eliciting Your Prospects' Buying Strategy

Ask the right questions if you're going to find the right answers.
—Vanessa Redgrave

Every outcome that we achieve and every decision that we make is a result of our internal processing strategy. What this means is that when we encounter a stimulus – usually an external one such as when you hear or see something – our brains use a strategy of processing to decipher the information we have received or make sense of the experience we have been through and then reach a conclusion. The conclusion we arrive at will determine the decision we make, which in turn controls how we react and respond to that given situation. This process consists of sequences of thoughts that are generated based on our knowledge, belief system, experiences, and other factors that affect us emotionally and logically. It follows that, with this understanding of how decisions are made and, in our context, our prospects' internal buying strategy, we can tailor our sales script to match their buying pattern. This helps them understand our plan better and increases the chances of a successful sales closing.

There are two ways to elicit a strategy: you can do it when the person is actually running it, or you can do it by asking the person to recall and share with you a previous occasion when the strategy was used. In a sales context, the latter will be more feasible and usually produces better results. This is because, like all behaviours, our buying behaviours rarely change. From a psychological point of view, it is accepted that people's behaviour, attitudes, habits, and beliefs are entrenched during the early years of their life. No changes – or at best, very minimal changes – will occur later in life unless we go through some traumatic or life-changing event. Once you found out how prospects bought a similar product in the past, you can fit your product features and benefits into their strategy and repeat it back to them – same strategy, different product. It's like a filling-in-the-blanks exercise!

In order to elicit a strategy, we use a series of questions aimed at extracting the primary reasons, considerations, and factors influencing their buying decision. There is no standard set of questions for this, as they all depend on the type of products you are selling and the prospect's previous buying experience. However, the following are some commonly used and effective questions that you could use as a guide when designing your own.

- "What made you buy that insurance plan in the past?"
- "Above all, what factors affected you the most in your decision to buy? Meeting certain needs? Peace of mind? Affordable premium?"
- "Did anyone else have a say in that decision process besides you?"
- "What were your main objections or concerns when you bought that plan?"
- "What do you like or not like about that plan?"
- "Were you satisfied with the seller? What were the things you liked or disliked about him or her?"
- "In hindsight, were there any additional features or benefits you would prefer the product to have?"
- "Do you like the plan now? Which benefits do you think are the most important to you now?

While probing for information, be careful not to be overzealous in your questioning and turn it into an interrogation session. You can always use it as an ice-breaker or opening speech, or you can do it during the fact-finding session when you are learning more about your prospect. For example, you could start by saying, "Dear prospect, if you don't mind, I am just wondering if you have bought such a plan in your past and what made you buy the plan?" You could explain that the purpose of these questions is to help you understand the prospect's needs and priorities to help you find a plan that best suit and serve his or her interest. If your prospect tells you the reason was "because of the high protection it provides" and the prospect doesn't seem to mind the higher premium, you should be able to infer that protection is the priority and that premium amount will not be a hindrance. If the prospect mentions a spouse's involvement, that should tell you that you may need the spouse to be present at the meeting too so that you can find out and take into consideration his or her needs as well.

Why ask about the previous seller? Knowing what your prospect liked or disliked about the seller will help you avoid behaving in ways that your prospect does not like. For instance, if your prospect complains that the seller spoke too fast, you should slow down your presentation. If your prospect is not satisfied with the after-sales service, you should provide assurance by emphasizing your professional after-sales sales service. If your prospect says that in hindsight he or she would have purchased some other product that offered some particular features, you could then suggest a product your company offers which includes those benefits.

Why ask your prospect if they like the plan they bought earlier? The reason is that most people will not realize what they value most about a plan until they have had it for some time. There is a good chance that your prospects will have a better answer to what they expect from such a plan now, and armed with this information, you will be able find the perfect product for them.

The Assumption-Questioning Technique

What about prospects who have not had a chance to buy the type of products you are trying to sell them? How do we elicit their strategy? For prospects who are hearing about such products for the first time, you may use the *assumption technique*. This technique requires foresight on the part of your prospects: they will have to imagine themselves having already bought your product. By placing themselves in the future, figuratively speaking, they should be able to share with you what is important to them and what is not.

Words or phrases that are particularly useful for this technique are "let's say", "what if", "as if", "for example", "imagine", and "assuming". Examples below will give you an idea of how these questions can be structured.

- "I understand that you have not come across such a plan before. However, just imagine that you have such a plan now. What are the features you will find most beneficial to you and your family?"
- "Let's say you have already bought a similar plan to this. What features do you think would have been the determining factors in your decision to buy?"
- "Assuming you already owned such plans, what expectations would you have of your seller's after-sales services?

Your prospect might reveal that if he owned this plan, he would most probably find a medical card with comprehensive coverage most useful. Perhaps the feature that provides him the most peace of mind is the high sum assured payable upon total and permanent disability. Maybe he expects the seller not only to be knowledgeable about his products but also to be a person who will make the extra effort to keep in touch with his prospects.

As you can see, these probing questions will lead your prospects to put themselves in the future as if they already had such plans. This will help them clarify their own needs and wants and reveal them to you. This in turn allows you to find a suitable product for them or to customize one to meet their requirements – producing a win-win outcome.

> *He who asks a question is a fool for five minutes; he who*
> *does not ask a question remains a fool forever.*
> —*Chinese proverb*

Chapter Seven

Your Prospects' Motivation Direction

Motivation is the art of getting people to do what you want them to do because they want to do it.
—Dwight D. Eisenhower

Our motivation direction determines the types of impetus that are likely to move us to take action. It is an important aspect of how we motivate ourselves. Are you motivated by something you want to *achieve* or by something you want to *avoid*? In NLP, we term this "move towards" or "move away from" motivation; you either move towards a pleasure or away from a pain. This motivation system has a powerful influence over what decisions we make in our lives and whether we take any action.

Of course, no one belongs completely to one extreme or the other. At some level, if the reward is big enough or the consequences are bad enough, everyone will move towards or away from something. However, most people tend to be dominated by one of the directions or the other. Because of this, we will be able to build rapport or communicate with them more effectively by conversing with them in their own motivation direction.

How do we determine a person's motivation direction? You could simply ask a general question such as "What do you want in life, job, or career?" The person will tell you either *what they want* or *what they don't want*. For example, "I *want* a big house with large rooms, surrounded by nature and fresh, clean air" or "I *don't want* a house that is too cramped or hot, and it should be away from pollution." These descriptions could be referring to the exact same house, although they are expressed in very different ways. The former is clearly a *move-towards* motivation and the latter is a *move-away-from* motivation.

The same thing can be done with your prospects when you sell them an insurance product. You could ask them for instance, "What would make you consider buying an insurance plan?" and a *move-towards* prospect might say, "*I want* peace of mind knowing that my family is well protected," while a *move-away-from* prospect might say, "I *don't want* my family to have financial issues when something bad happens to me." Once you have identified their motivation direction, you can tailor your sales pitch by focusing more on the benefits they will gain if they buy and the problems they may face if they don't. Below are some examples of how this can be done.

Move Towards

- "With this insurance plan, you will be able to enjoy life knowing that you have all the protection you need for yourself and your family."
- "The maturity value in this plan will give you the money you need to have a great retirement."
- "Your family will thank you for planning ahead for them."
- "Imagine that all your medical bills are covered for you in the event that you fall ill. How relieved would you feel?"

Move Away

- "Without this insurance plan, you will not be able to enjoy your life, because you will have constant worry about not being sufficiently covered."

- "Retirement is more costly than most people expect. If you don't have such plans to supplement your retirement fund, you may have a tough time in the future."
- "If some mishap were to happen to you, aren't you worried that your family would feel disappointed at you for not planning ahead?"
- "Just think about how frustrated you would be if you – in addition to dealing with your illness – still had to fork out a large amount of money for medical bills."

What if you are not able to discover your prospect's motivation direction? Or, what if your prospect speaks in a way that includes both directions? "I want a house that has a beautiful garden surrounded by greenery. But I wouldn't want it to be too large, as I don't want to spend too much time cleaning up the house". For such prospects, you can try mixing both moving-towards and away-from directions in your sales presentation. It's like using both parts of the "carrot and stick" motivation simultaneously.

Using both directions is especially useful in a group setting, where the chances are you have more than one type of audience present. Covering both directions will ensure that neither one is left out. A good rule of thumb is to mix both directions in your presentation when you are uncertain to which one your prospect belongs.

Chapter Eight

Pacing, Leading, and Anchoring

If everybody is moving forward together, then success takes care of itself.
—Henry Ford

Pacing and Leading

Earlier, we explored how we could pace our prospects by mirroring and matching them verbally and non-verbally. Once both your and your prospect's movement starts to synchronize or move together effortlessly, you can be said to have "locked" on to each other. It means that your mirroring and matching has been executed so successfully that both of you are tuned in to each other's mental and physical states – an indication of good rapport. The next step is to lead your prospect to a more open and receptive mind-set towards your product.

Leading is especially useful when dealing with an uninterested prospect. For example, the unkeen prospect may lean back in the chair with arms folded and legs crossed, or may turn the body sideways as if preparing to leave as soon as you are finished. In this case, you should pace the prospect by mirroring body language, also folding your arms and crossing your legs while you lean back in your chair. Do this for about two to three minutes. Once you feel that you have reached a level of rapport with your prospect and you have "locked" on to each other, gradually move forwards towards your prospect and lean over the table, assuming a more interested and eager posture. You will be amazed when your prospect follows suit.

The way we carry ourselves on the outside affects our feelings and attitudes on the inside. A good example is when you smile, you naturally feel happier, even at a time when you have no reasons to feel that way. This is because you simply cannot feel sad when you have a wide, silly grin on your face – the mind and body connection. By assuming this posture, your prospect will start to feel more enthusiastic and receptive towards your presentation.

To test if you have a good "lock" on your client, try intentionally but subtly changing your posture or body language, such as from crossed leg to uncrossed, to see if your client follows. If the client does, he or she is likely to be considerably receptive to you now, and leading the conversation becomes easy. Constantly check to ensure that your client is still "locked" on. If not, re-initiate the leading process by mirroring and matching again in both verbal and non-verbal ways.

Pacing and Leading a Group

Pacing and leading one prospect is the same as doing it with a group. However, you need to do it one small group at a time in clusters. The audiences within these group clusters tend to mirror each other. If one person crosses his or her arms, a few may do it, and the rest will follow. If one person starts talking, the rest should follow.

Do not try to pace and lead the whole group at once; you simply can't. Use the "divide and conquer" strategy: focus, pace, and lead one cluster at a time. When speaking to a cluster with the majority crossing their arms, pace them by folding your arms, and then lead them by slowly letting your hands down after speaking to them a while. If it doesn't work, attempt it again until you have succeeded. You may not get every single person in the cluster to follow. That's fine. So long as most of them are with you now, you will still make a significant impact.

Besides pacing and leading the group through body language, you could also do it verbally through the intonation, speed, and volume of your speech. Always try to gauge the sentiment of your audiences before you start. Running up the stage and shouting *"Aren't' we happy to be here today?"* will irritate a group or audience with low energy. If you have a quiet and non-enthusiastic group, start slowly and speak with a moderate tone, match their moods and energy level, and gradually lift them up. Try steadily and gradually increasing your voice, injecting some humour and exciting facts. Start by getting a few people to laugh at your jokes and participate in your presentation by asking them to stand up and answer questions. Remember: mood and energy are contagious; the light-hearted mood and enthusiasm you evoke in a few audience members will eventually spread to your entire group.

Anchoring

In NLP "anchoring" refers to the process of linking an internal response with some external or internal trigger so that the response may be quickly elicited. Anchoring is reminiscent to the conditioning technique used by Pavlov to create an association between the hearing of a bell and salivation in dogs. Pavlov sounded a bell as the animal was given food. The animals salivated when they saw the food. After a repetitive association between the bell and the food was established, the bell alone elicited salivation even when food was not given.

In NLP this type of associative conditioning has been expanded to include links between other aspects of experience than purely environmental cues and behavioural responses. An object may become an anchor for a particular emotion. For instance, a photo or souvenir may be an anchor for certain memories; a touch on the arm may become an anchor for certain emotions; or clenching your fist may be an anchor for a state of excitement or confidence. These states are usually evoked unconsciously in our daily life. However, the great news is that a person may consciously choose to establish and retrigger these associations for his or her own benefit.

In other words, anchors are stimuli that evoke states of mind such as thoughts and emotions. Some anchors are voluntary, such as you touching your left knuckle, while others are involuntary, such as the smell of bread taking you back to your childhood. A song or tune may remind you of a certain person. A touch can bring back memories and the past states. These anchors work automatically, and you may not be aware of the triggers.

Establishing an anchor means producing the stimulus (the anchor) when the resourceful state is being experienced so that the resourceful state is paired to the anchor. And in the case of your prospects, you pair the stimulus to a state of mind that you want them to experience, such as love for family. For example, every time you mention how much the prospect's family depends on him or her to take care of them, you gently touch his or her upper arm. After doing this a few times, you will have paired being touched on his arm to love for family. You will then trigger this feeling again when you finally go for a close. Your prospect's feelings of love for his or her family will help lead to a decision to buy.

Visual Anchors

Anchoring can be done more effectively if you first try to find out your prospect's preferred representational system – visual, auditory, or kinaesthetic. You can use visual anchors to associate the required state of mind on your visually-oriented prospects; these anchors can be external or internal. For example, you could use a picture of a loving family to anchor the feelings of love and care in your prospect. Every time you need to evoke this emotion, simply show the prospect the picture again. However, ensure that this external anchor is always available for you to use; otherwise, you could instead set up an internal anchor by asking your prospect to visualize a mental picture of his or her family.

Auditory Anchors

You can use a sound as an anchor for auditory-oriented prospects. You can tap the table, snap your fingers, or even inflect your voice.

For example, when it's time to anchor your prospect, you gently tap on the sales material you have been using. You could also lower your pitch and slow down your speech when you want to anchor certain phrases such as "Think about your family". Say it in an earnest and deliberate way to evoke the emotions you want. Repeat this until you feel the connection is established.

Kinaesthetic Anchors

Kinaesthetic prospects are easy to anchor, because they are highly responsive to touch. You can either touch them lightly with your finger, or pass them the sales material you have been using and ask them to hold it and look at it. Do this a few times, and every time you want to elicit the response you have anchored, you use the trigger again.

Original Anchors

Original anchors refer to gestures that hold special meaning to us. They are not created by the methods we have discussed above or by another person. These gestures or anchors are original to us – something we have developed unconsciously over the years. We may tap the table when we are trying to assert a point, clasp our hands when we feel happy, and so on. If we can spot these special gestures in our prospects, we will be able to use them to our benefit later.

Let's say your prospect invariably clenches his fist when speaking about how the importance of his or her family. You clench your fist too when emphasizing a feature that is important to the family. Pay close attention to your prospects at the beginning of the conversation and try to make them talk more by asking questions. They will leak out their personal anchors, and that will prove invaluable to you in your presentation later.

Chapter Nine

Handling Objections by Pacing and Reframing

There are no facts, only interpretations.
—Friedrich Nietzsche

The Feel, Felt, and Found Approach

The first thing we learn in a sales career is that objections are inevitable. In fact, they are a necessary step towards closing any sale. Contrary to belief, objections are often not a sign of disinterest but rather an indication of lack of understanding or conviction about the benefits offered by your product. They are your prospect's way of saying, "I need more information!" or "I need you to convince me that your product does in fact benefit me!" Uninterested prospects, on the contrary, will not even be bothered to raise objections; they will usually try to reject you on the pretence that they have fully understood everything and have decided not to buy. Without objections from the prospect, you will have no way of unravelling why you got "no" for an answer.

The first step to effectively handle objections is to pace your prospects in their views and feelings, and this can be done by applying the *Feel, Felt, and Found* approach to handling objections. This is how it works. First, you tell your prospects that you understand how they *feel*. Then you follow by saying that many other customers of yours also *felt* the same way, but after your explanation, they all *found* that what they believed may not be true after all. For example, if you prospect tells you that he or she doesn't like the product because it's too expensive, you respond by saying, "I understand how you *feel*. This plan may seem to have a higher premium in comparison to others. Many of my clients also *felt* that way initially. However, after I showed them other benefits, they *found* that that the premium charges are actually very reasonable."

What we are attempting to achieve here is to let prospects feel that we empathize with them. By saying "I understand how you *feel*", we show we are listening to them and that we understand their concerns. When we say, "Many of my customers also *felt* that way", we are telling them that they are not alone; many people also felt the same way as they did. And finally, when we say, "However, after I showed them some information, they found that the plan actually benefits them", we are leveraging on other customers' favourable opinions and decisions about our product – the "herd mentality".

The Feel, Felt, and Found approach is unquestionably a kinaesthetic-oriented technique. So how do we ensure that equally good results will ensue for prospects with visual and auditory modes of thinking? It's simple. All you have to do is to use predicates that match your prospects' representation system. For a visually-oriented prospect, you could say, "I can *see* your concerns. I *see* that the premium rates seem a little on the high side. In fact, many of my customers thought the same too. However, after I gave them an overall *view* of the plan's benefits, they changed their *perspective* and could *see* how the plan benefits them in a much better way". Similarly, use auditory-friendly predicates with prospects who are in auditory mode. You could say for example, "I *hear* what you are saying. Many customers have *told* me the same thing, but after I explained the benefits in detail, they responded that this *sounds* like a good plan to have". Notice how I have changed the predicates in the preceding two examples while maintaining the essence of the original message? Be creative in forming your sentences. There are no strict rules on how it should be done. With a bit of conscious practice, you will be able to do this unconsciously very soon.

Reframing

The Feel, Felt and Found approach requires the seller to change the prospect's opinion of the product. We call this *reframing* in NLP. Basically, it means changing the meaning of something or experiences of someone by helping that person see it from a different point of view. In effect, you help the person see the same thing in a different context, thereby changing the person's perception and along with it, his or her feelings and decisions and, ultimately, the outcome of your relationship with that person. For instance, speaking about the fact that everyone will die sooner or later will get you kicked out from your neighbour's birthday party, but the saying the same will not be frowned upon if it's mentioned during an insurance-product sales presentation. Similarly, albeit on a more extreme note, wearing a skeleton costume to attend a funeral is very different from dressing in one for a Halloween party.

In insurance, reframing is highly effective in turning a prospect's negative or neutral mind-set to a more positive and receptive attitude towards your product. This is done by simply turning an objection into an opportunity for a sale. In other words, you turn what appears to be a product drawback from your prospect's point of view to a benefit or advantage. Below are some examples of how we can use the reframing technique in our presentation.

Negative Response	Reframe	New Perspective
"I don't have money to buy this now."	"You are not buying something; you are investing for financial security."	Instead of buying, the prospect now sees it as an investment for peace of mind.
"I am still young now. Why the hurry to buy?"	"You should buy now when you are young and healthy, because you can't buy it if you are old and sick."	Instead of being an excuse for procrastination, the young age of the prospect is now the reason for buying.

"I am healthy. I don't need insurance."	"You certainly don't need insurance when you are healthy. You buy it when you are healthy and need it when you are not."	The prospect understands that insurance is to be bought when one is healthy and *for* times when one is not.
"I have plenty of money. I don't need insurance protection."	"Insurance is there to help pay your medical bills in the event that you fall ill so that you can preserve your wealth."	Now the prospect sees insurance as a protection for wealth. Let insurance take care of the medical bills so he or she can enjoy money.
"I am on a tight budget and worried that I can't continue paying later."	"Assuming your income has been slashed by ten per cent, will you still be able to live on?"	The prospect will realize that most people are able to make adjustments to their monthly expenditures once they have committed to something important like an insurance plan. Savings can be made by cutting down on unnecessary expenditures.
"I am concerned about the long payment term and not being able to commit to it."	"Like paying for our mortgage or car loan instalment, once committed we find the discipline to complete the payments."	Most people pay up their housing and car loans without issues once they have committed to them. It's a matter of discipline.

"I don't need insurance."	"The question is not whether you need insurance but rather whether your loved ones need it?"	This switches the prospect's attention to the family instead of himself or herself. In this context, most would agree that their loved ones need it.
"It is too expensive."	"Good things don't come cheap."	This reminds your prospects that you have to pay for quality. By highlighting the benefits your plan offers over and above your rivals, you will convince them that they are paying for a good product.

Reframing is a skill that can be honed with enough practice. Try writing down some common objections thrown at you by your prospects and then reframing them. With some practice, it will come naturally during your presentation.

In sales, it's not what you say; it's how they perceive what you say.
—Jeffrey Gitomer

Mode Shifting

Have you ever met prospects who are so rigid and inflexible that no matter how tenable your answers to their objections are, they simply cannot be persuaded? In the previous chapters, you have learned that people don't see the world the same way we do. Facts and information are subject to people's interpretations and perceptions of the world, which in turn are based on their past exposures and experiences. As we know, our experiences become part of us, making it extremely difficult to change.

One way to deal with this is to change their points of view by switching the representation system through which they filter the information you are providing: this is called *mode shifting*. It simply means that if you are struggling to convince a visually-oriented prospect to see something from your point of view, try presenting the same information through an auditory mode.

For instance, if your prospects were once conned by an insurance agent into buying something that they didn't need, they may see all insurance agents in a bad light – dishonest and profit-minded. If your attempts to change their mind-set with brochures have been futile, try showing them a video of an insurance commercial presenting similar benefits instead. The combination of sounds and images engages both the auditory and visual senses, thus causing a shift in their mode of representation and ultimately their perspective.

Equally effective is to replace visual predicates you have been using for this prospect with predicates of other modes. Use the words *hear* and *listen*, or *feel* and *touch*, instead of *see* and *view*. This achieves the same effect in shifting the way they receive and process the same information.

It is not hard to understand that if a prospect's view of insurance has been tainted by a poor experience, he or she may never see it in a different light again. Just imagine that your prospects are seeing through a pair of glasses that are badly tainted and impossible to clean. With vision impeded and views obstructed, how could you possibility expect someone to see what you are presenting? Now, what if we help them understand what we are trying to show them by verbally explaining to them? Or by allowing them to touch and feel the information kinaesthetically? Remember to remain flexible in your strategies. If one method does not produce the results you want, try another.

Reframing for the Seller

Always remember that objections are a form of feedback from your prospects. Without them your meeting is non-productive, one-way communication. Many salespeople see objections as a negative response from their prospects – a type of rejection – which is simply not true. The reason they see it this way is because they see it in a negative light, taking the comments negatively rather than in a constructive way.

When a prospect says "Why is the premium so expensive?" he may be just interested in finding out more about how the product features justify the premium in comparison to similar products in the market. Unfortunately, some sellers may interpret it as a rejection and think that their prospect believes that their product is inferior in comparison to others. For this reason, it is very often the seller's mind-set that has to be changed. We need to "reframe" the meaning of objections in our mind's eye. In other words, we need to learn to see objections in a different light – as being *opportunities* rather than *obstacles*. Once you do that, you will learn to welcome objections, because you will view them as stepping stones towards a successful deal.

Chapter Ten

The Three-Step
BAA Closing Process

You miss 100 per cent of the shots you don't take.
—Michael Jordan

In this final chapter we will explore a powerful closing technique based the principles of NLP. Many salespeople hesitate or waver when they reach the final step of the sales process. They are afraid to broach the subject due to the fear of being rejected. But as Michael Jordan once said, "You miss 100 per cent of the shots you don't take." Despite the fact that there is no guaranteed success in every deal, there are ways or formulas, when applied, that provide a high chance of success. And after studying the ways many top sales performers clinch their deal, we discovered that they all have something in common in their approach. In NLP we call this their winning strategy. Winning strategies are methods employed by outstanding performers to achieve exceptional results in their area of endeavour. We study and emulate their formulas so that, by using them, anyone could also achieve similar results in those areas. And a closing formula that we will explore here is called the *BAA three-step closing*. BAA stands for "Benefit, Anchoring, Assumptive Closing".

B = Benefit

As your presentation is drawing to an end, all questions have been answered and all objections handled. You start your closing by first doing a recap of the benefits for your prospects. List them one by one, and remind them of how it could benefit them or their family. Keep it succinct. To your surprise, most prospects will have forgotten some or most of the benefits by the end of the presentation, and this hampers their ability to make decisions. However, summarizing and explaining to them the benefits alone would not suffice. You will need to create the impetus – the drive – that would push them to make a decision, which leads us to the next step: anchoring.

A = Anchoring

We have learned earlier that emotions or feelings can be anchored with certain physical gestures, or even with words or images, and can similarly be evoked once the anchor is activated. If the common saying is true that "Buying is an emotional process", it follows that your prospects must experience a kind of "emotional jolt" in order for them to cross the boundary from "I want to think about it" to "Let's signed up now". These strong emotions that you anchored in your prospect during the course of your presentation, be it the love felt for family or the fear of high medical costs, can be triggered while doing the first step of repeating the benefits. Let's say you have anchored a feeling of love in your prospect and the trigger is a picture of a happy family, show the same picture again while taking the prospect through the benefits. If the same feelings are anchored with certain words, use such words again. Done properly, you will reinvigorate a dull prospect and galvanize him or her into taking action. This is a simple yet highly effective technique in eliciting the emotional response necessary for fuelling a buying decision.

A = Assumptive Closing

The last step in the three-step closing process is *assumptive closing*. What this basically means is that the seller bypasses questions like "So, do you want to buy my insurance plan?" which would inevitably put both parties in an awkward situation. Instead he jumps straight into an assumption that the prospect has already decided to buy by asking, for example, "Would you like to pay the premium in monthly or yearly mode?" This bold move is crucial in closing a deal, as it eliminates all doubts and leaves no room for indecisiveness. It forces the prospects to decide how they feel about the product and stop endlessly weighing its pros and cons. Coupled with the "emotional push" trigged by the anchoring process, you can be assured of a done deal.

There are no limits as to how you can do an assumptive closing. Below are some of the top performers' favourites.

Payment:

- "Would you like to pay by cash, credit card, or auto-debit?"
- "Would you like to pay the premiums in yearly or monthly mode?"

Ask for personal information:

- "Can I have your full name and address, please?"
- "Who would the beneficiary be?"
- "May I have your date of birth, please?"

Recommendation:

- "I recommend this premium amount. Are you fine with it?"
- "I would like to add this extra benefit to your basic plan. What do you think?"
- "I suggest you to buy this amount of sum assured. Any opinion?"

How an assumptive closing should be worded also depends very much on the type of product you are selling, so try different ways and find the ones that suit your prospects and product the best results. Once you have mastered this three-step BAA closing process, you will be amazed by how powerful it is.

Conclusion

No skills can be mastered without rigorous and committed practice. The same is true for the techniques you have learned in this book. As the saying goes, practice makes perfect. Any skills can be perfected with enough practice, and anyone can be an adept insurance seller in NLP with the right devotion. Like riding a bicycle, you will have to do it consciously at the beginning. This is when you are getting a feel of things, but after enough practice, it all comes naturally.

The same goes for NLP techniques. At the start you will be consciously applying the techniques, and you will need some perseverance to stick to it on a daily basis. But before you know it, you will get the hang of it and execution will become seamless. Like all other things, it becomes a habit and the natural way you sell and build rapport. Start using this powerful tool, and see how it instantly brings dramatic improvements to your sales performance. Don't wait. Start today! Start now!

Printed in the United States
By Bookmasters